RUN YOUR LIFE

TAKING CONTROL OF YOUR LIFE AND YOUR BUSINESS

RAY YOUNG

Copyright © 2024 by Ray Young

All rights reserved.

No part of this book may be reproduced in any form or by any electronic or mechanical means, including information storage and retrieval systems, without written permission from the author, except for the use of brief quotations in a book review.

INTRODUCTION

There are only two kinds of people in the world. Those who have to make all their own mistakes and those who can learn from the mistakes of people.

There are only two kinds of people in the world. Those who have to learn everything on their own and those who can learn from the experiences of others.

If you are the second kind of person this book is for you!

Wait! This book is about running – but it is not ABOUT running. It is how running changed my life – and how the lessons I learned from running can change your life!

These are real lessons learned the real way that made a real difference.

1

START WITH WHY!

One day, everything in my life changed.
No, that's not an overstatement.
I know you've heard it before and it seems dramatic but it is literally the truth.

YOU NEVER KNOW what a day will hold.
You never know what changes will come in just one day. It was 5:45 in the morning. My wife and I were still in bed asleep when we were awakened by our daughter saying, "I'm headed to practice. Y'all have a good day." This had happened before. It was a daily experience. Every week day she went to cross country practice. This morning was different. I had a question that I've not asked before.

I ASKED HER, "Who's running with you?"

SHE SAID, "WHAT DO YOU MEAN?"

. . .

STILL HALF ASLEEP I RESPONDED, "It's a simple question. When you go run, who runs with you?"

YOU SEE, my 15-year-old daughter was part of her high school cross-country team. She was on her way to practice and I simply wanted to know who else was running. She said again, "Dad, what do you mean?"

I SAID, "It's simple. What other athletes are running?"

FINALLY SHE RESPONDED, "Everyone else's in afternoon practice. But since I have other things to do after school, I have to practice in the morning."

I ASKED HER, "Does Coach run with you?"

SHE SAID NO.

I SAID, "Does he drive by and check on you?"

SHE SAID NO.

. . .

"Wait a minute," I said. The response was out of my mouth and I was out of bed in an instant. "Wait just a second. I'll go with you."

I thought to myself, *there is no way my 15-year-old daughter will run around town at six o'clock in the morning all by herself.* So I jumped up, put on some shorts, and drove her to the gym where she met her coach. He told her what route to run, and she took off. As she ran, I followed her.

The next morning I set the alarm. I was ready before she was ready. I took her to school again. This was the morning that my whole life was going to change. I had no idea HOW MUCH it was going to change. As she was running, I thought to myself you need to get out and run with her. And then I laughed. You see, I had lost 20 pounds. So I was down to 255 pounds. I thought there is no way I could run with her. But I knew I had to. So the next morning I took her to school, dropped her off and I drove to the first corner of her route. That is when it started. I started running. I would run till I could see her and then turn around and run back to my Suburban. Drive to the next corner and do the same thing. I repeated corner by corner of that route day after day, week after week until I could run the whole time and see her for the whole four-mile run.

Here is an important fact you need to know. This gives the context for how this was life changing. I have always HATED running. It was one of those things I had to do in school and I promised myself I would never do this again.

. . .

IN JUST ONE DAY, everything changed. I don't mean just in my health. I don't mean just in my fitness. I don't mean just in my running. I mean this literally running changed my whole life. It changed me physically. It changed me mentally. It changed my diet. It changed my relationships. It changed my businesses. It changed my faith. It changed EVERYTHING!

LEARNING to run changed the way I approach life and business.

I SHARE the story with you to encourage you, to inspire you, to equip you, and to motivate you to start. We all have things inside of us. Things that we believe we want to do. Things we believe we must do. Things that we say we're going to do one day, or someday. Friend, I've got news for you. Maybe it's the first time you've heard it or maybe it's just a reminder, *Someday* is not a day on your calendar.

I DON'T KNOW how many things you've done. But I know that I've been guilty of saying I'm going to start this Monday. Of course, I never said which Monday. Monday of next week, or the next week after that, or the next month. We are good at putting off starting. We easily become PROs at PROcrastination! It may be that you say *I'm not even sure why, I just felt like I have to, I need to, I want to.* I feel like I have to overcome this bad habit. I want to be a better spouse or parent. I need to get control of my finances. I should start working out. It would be good if I saved some money. One day I am going to start my own business. Someday I will ask for a raise.

THE PROBLEM IS that it does not feel like a MUST.

YOU DON'T HAVE to know why to start, but you *must* discover it.

AS LONG AS you can put it off – it is not really important to you.

LAO TZU SAID,

"The journey of 1000 miles begins with just one step."

Today I encourage you not to think about it, not to put it off. In fact, as much as I want you to read the rest of this book. If you need to, put it down right now and actually take action.

DON'T JUST DREAM. Don't just think. Don't just plan. Don't just work out all of the possibilities. You need to actually take action today. You may say, *but I'm not ready. I don't have a plan. I don't have the resources. There's someone who is better.* You can go through all of the excuses but I want to tell you this - *If you start right now, you will figure it out as you go!* If now is not the right time, then you tell me, when would now be a good time to start? There will never be the perfect time.

There is no such thing as the perfect plan. The setting and opportunity will never be exactly as you desire. If you wait for those things you will forever be waiting.

RECOGNIZE THIS, there are opportunities that never come again. This is a moment in time you will never have again. If you can figure out why this is not the right time, I'll suggest to you if you can put it off, you will continue to put it off until it's too late. The most powerful and common reason to not start now is fear. When I say that it is the most powerful you must understand this –

FEAR ONLY HAS THE POWER THAT YOU GIVE IT!

Fear is looking at the future and imagining all of the things that could go wrong. It is playing a negative "what if" game. With the same imagination you could look to the future and see a positive outcome. You could play the positive "what if" game. What if it did work out? What if it meets my expectations? What if it exceeds my expectations? What if this is the best decision... the best action... the best thing I have done to this point in my life?

THE TRUTH IS the same for every single one of us - we were made for action. Just consider your body. Stand up. Everything points forward. Your eyes look forward. Your nose points forward. You face is front facing. Your feet point forward. Your knees point forward. You were made to move forward! We were not made to sit still. We were not made to stay in one place. We were not made to live at one level in life. And yet, it's easy just to fall into the trap. It's easy to settle for the status quo, the monotonous. You do the same thing day after day, week after week, month after month, year after year, and nothing changes.

Saying that nothing changes is not exactly true. The truth is something does change. The dream inside of you. Inaction changes your belief in yourself. Procrastination changes your view of the future. Your ability to perform decreases. Your personal and professional growth ceases. You start decreasing. The ability to improve, to make a difference in your life, in your family, in your friends, at work, whatever you're involved in - it diminishes.

ANY PLAN IS BETTER THAN WAITING FOR THE PERFECT PLAN

You need a plan. You don't have to have it all planned out. Here is the beautiful thing about that - as you go to work, when you start, when you take action, moving towards that destination, making the goal a reality, living that dream... It's just like planning a vacation or just like shopping for Christmas -the best part is usually the work you do to get there. That's the most meaningful part.

Have you ever had that experience? You are so excited about Christmas morning. You have thought. You have planned. You have shopped. You have wrapped. The gifts are under the Christmas tree. The time finally comes. The paper is ripped off and the gifts are appreciated. They are looked at and then it's kind of like you've got this letdown. You had everything built up in your mind. You have worked so hard. You prepared. Then it was all over in an instant. Now there's an important lesson in that little illustration.

IF YOU CANNOT ENJOY the journey, you will not enjoy the destination.

TOO MANY OF us put off enjoying life and do not enjoy the process. Enjoying the grind, enjoying the growth, enjoying today. Looking forward to the future. You remember doing it. I can remember when I was in junior high, I could not wait to get to high school. When I finally got to high school I said I couldn't wait till I was old enough to get my driver's license. I can't wait till I have my own car. I can't wait till I have a job. I can't wait till I go to college. I can't wait to have this freedom. I can't wait till I graduate. I can't wait till I get that first big-boy job. I can't wait till I get a raise. I can't wait for my vacation. I can't wait to get married. I can't wait to get have kids. I can't wait till they can walk. I can't wait till they're going to school. I can't wait till they graduate.

It is easy for us to fall in the state of always putting off life. I can't wait till I achieve this goal. I can't wait to buy that house or drive that car or whatever.

If you're always putting off life, you're never fully living life.

If you can't enjoy today, you will not enjoy tomorrow. Do you know why? You need a vision. You need a destination. You need a goal. You need a dream. Again, you do not need to know every step. Know the first step. Refuse to take another meaningless step.

. . .

WHAT IS A MEANINGLESS STEP? When you actually start – maybe it is starting a business – the easy thing to do is take a lot of steps that feel good but really are not a start. They are meaningless steps. You have no idea how many business start-ups have come to me for coaching. They are excited about all that they have done. As I ask what all they have done so I know what the next steps are I find out something that is disheartening. They have taken a lot of steps – but they are not the right steps. They have spent countless hours designing and redesigning the "perfect business card." Some have ordered them and then decided that they could do better. Some have spent money having a graphic designer create their business cards. They say things like, "every business needs a great website. The website is the first impression. You never get a second chance to make a first impression. So they research every kind of website. Then they research competitors websites. They sketch out their own website. They start building a website after spending hours deciding what they perfect website URL is. Then they pay someone to make a website. They have a marketing plan along with extensive marketing materials. They have done EVERYTHING but the actual business. They have spent so much money laying all of the groundwork. They have WASTED so much time getting it just right. They have doubted themselves over and over. Played the "what if" game endlessly. All of the activity. No business.

I WORKED with a man who dreamed of opening a BBQ restaurant. He talked to all the people seeking best ideas. He researched all of the competition so that he could be the best at everything anyone else was doing. He perfected recipes. Then he improved the perfect. He had logos made.

He designed the menus. He had the menus printed. He designed the pit for smoking the meat. He bought land. He prepared the site for construction. He got water and sewer in place. He literally spent years working on the business and never sold any BBQ. He never served a single guest.

WHAT IS YOUR BBQ STORY?

NOT ONLY DO we have internal struggles. We have plenty of excuses. There are more than enough distracting actions. In addition there are outside forces. Let me illustrate with another running story.

SILENCE THE NEGATIVITY

You have got to learn to ignore the haters. I remember in those early days of running there was one particular route we would run. It seemed like every time we ran down this road, there would be a man sitting on his front porch. My daughter was always ahead of me and he always had something to say about it.

"Hey, old man, you sure are slow."

"Hey, old man, you better run faster. She's getting away."

"Hey, old man, it'd be better if you were driving a car."

The first couple of times it really bothered me. I would spend the rest of the run and sometimes the rest of the day thinking about it. I'm not good enough. I'm not fast enough. Who am I kidding? Why am I even doing this? The questions went on and on and on. It was becoming a real problem. Then one day it hit me. It's easy to sit on the porch and take shots at people who are actually doing it. Think about that.

There are several things I want to encourage you to do.

First - Do Not Become A Hater.

Never be the person on the porch telling other people they should give up or that they can't do it. They're not good enough. They're not fast enough. *There's enough discouragement in the world.* Don't be one of the discouragers. Don't rain on someone's parade.

The truth about that guy was he could not have run if he wanted to. I was overweight, but he literally weighed more than twice what I weighed. He could not have done it. If you let the haters get in your head, you give them control. So first do not become a hater.

Second - Ignore the haters.

The voice of a hater, a doubter, a discourager is only powerful if you give it that power. Do not listen to that voice. Do not give their voice your consent!

Eleanor Roosevelt said, "No one can make you feel inferior without your consent."

Of course, it is hard. Listening to the opposing voice is harder. When we listen to the haters we let them have power over us. We let them control our goals, our determination, and our progress. So fight the fight!

Third – Talk to yourself don't listen to yourself

The question is whose voice is going to be loudest, strongest and most important to you? You have to talk to yourself. You have to develop your mindset. You have to drown out the other voices with your own voice.

I LEARNED – after a lot of work – to control my mind. When I heard an internal or external voice I took action. When I heard a present or past voice I responded. I took a verse from one of my favorite books in the Bible and actually practiced it.

PHILIPPIANS 4:8 SAYS, "Whatever is true, whatever is noble, whatever is right, whatever is pure, whatever is lovely, whatever is admirable, if anything is excellent, if anything is praiseworthy, think on such things."

I REMEMBER DISTINCTLY READING that early one morning and asking myself what difference it would make if I actually did it. I memorized the verse by using the first letter of each of the key words: TNRP LAEP. True. Noble. Right. Pure. Lovely. Admirable. Excellent. Praiseworthy. When one of those voices started in my head or outside of it I took control of my mind. When you are focused and intent you can control your mind! I would start with great intensity – either saying the letters in my head or sometimes out loud. I would repeat them rapidly and intensely over and over. I would move my body in a strong way as I repeated them. As I pushed everything else out I would begin to slow down my cadence. T N R P L A E P Once my mind had broken the other cycle I would say the whole word - True. Noble. Right. Pure. Lovely.

Admirable. Excellent. Praiseworthy. Repeat this over and over. When I had complete control of my mind I would begin to ask what is true? What is noble? What is right? On and on.

Tell yourself that you are growing. You are making progress. You are getting better. It is worth it. It does matter and you keep pushing. Push yourself and when you feel like you can't go on, when you feel like you can't take another step when you feel like you can't handle any more problems, stick with it just a little bit longer. You will have that breakthrough. You will get there. If you can learn anything from my running, the first thing I want you to learn is you have to start!

Fourth – **Recognize they are behind you!**

Have you ever thought about it? If someone is hating on you, if someone is telling you any of those messages or any of the messages like them, remember this - no one ahead of you will ever belittle you. It's only the people who are on the sidelines. It's only the people who are behind you. And so if you have people who like to take their shots, remember this. They are behind you. They are not even in the race. They are not even doing.

At work don't worry about them. Ignore them. Push them out. You do not have to literally push them out – just push out those voices. Then the second push is this – what you have you got to do is push yourself. The voices outside are tough.

. . .

THERE IS a voice that is more challenging to silence. It is the voice inside. You know it. You know the voice inside your head. You know the things you say to yourself. You know how to tear yourself down. You know the doubt. You know the questions. As hard as it is to block the outside voices, it is many times harder to block the inside voice. It is also much more important. *It is absolutely vital that you don't listen to yourself, but you learn to talk to yourself.*

MAKE IT YOURS!

What is my **real "why"** for the change I say I want—and what would make it a *must* instead of a *maybe*?

Where am I currently living in **procrastination** ("Monday... someday... when things calm down")—and what has it cost me so far?

What **fear-based "what if"** story do I keep rehearsing—and what is the **positive "what if"** I need to practice instead?

What "meaningless steps" am I taking (busy work that feels productive)—and what is the **first real step** I need to take?

If I started today, what would I do in the **next 24 hours** that proves I'm serious?

2

GET A PARTNER

If you want to go fast, go alone. If you want to go far go together.

One of the most important things I learned from running is that a partner is necessary.

You have to be careful who you spend time with. No one will have a greater impact on your life than the five people you spend the most time with.

It has often been repeated, five years from now you will be exactly the same person you are today except for the books you read and the five people you spend the most time with. Your eating habits will reflect those five closest friends. Your exercise habits will be the average of your five. Your sleep schedule will reflect that group. Your income will be about the average of the five people you spend the most time with. Your closest relationships – marriage or not, parenting style or no kids – they are all shaped by the inner circle. The habits you make are a part of your everyday life and the way you take care of your health.

Stop. Read that list again.

Your life in five years will be just what it is today except for the people you spend your time with and the books you read!

What you feed your mind. What you feed your body. The amount of exercise that you get. The habits that you make a part of your daily life. Just look at your five closest friends and know this - that is your future. Too many of us do things accidentally. We don't have any intention. We don't know our purpose. We don't know where we're going. And we're kind of just floating through life. Maybe that's where you are.

I lived my life that way for a long time. Running is one of the things that broke me out of that I decided that I wasn't going to settle for whatever happened. I wasn't going to just take things as they came. I made a decision that I wanted to control the things in my life that I could control. The truth was that I was in control of a lot more than I thought I was. Sometimes I was in control of a lot more than I wanted to be. I still wanted to be in control. I didn't like taking it as it came. I didn't like finding out how life would turn out if I continued to take the "let's just see what happens" approach.

It makes absolute sense. It's hard to actually put it into practice. If you spend the most of your time with people who aren't going where you want to go – you will not arrive at your destination. For me, if I spent most of my time with people who thought running was stupid, that running was ridiculous, that you had to be crazy to run, that it was going to damage your knees, that it was going to hurt your body - Then I would have had constant discouragement from running. So what I did was I surrounded myself with people who did love running, who thought it was great for your body who taught me the truth.

I did the research and found out the truth. If you are

running with proper form it doesn't hurt your knees. It doesn't hurt your hips. It is good for you. I've found from my own experience, that running made my body feel good. The things that hurt, hurt a lot less when I was running. So I surrounded myself with those people.

It's true for you. Whatever it is that you decide is really important in your life. Whatever it is that you decide, I am chasing after that. You must surround yourself with people who have common goals. Surround yourself with people who have a common purpose. They understand what gives meaning to your life. They will encourage you. They will push you. We all need encouragement. We all need a push.

When you CHOOSE the right people to keep close another great thing happens. You find people that you can encourage and push. You find encouragement and a push when you need it. You can encourage and push them when you're doing well. With the rhythm of life, it is rare for people to be in an identical state. Maybe one of them is struggling and you are doing well, or maybe one of them is doing well and you are struggling. When that happens you form a partnership - we are in this thing together.

The ancient scriptures say that

> "two are better than one because they get a greater return for their labor."

The phenomenon is called synergy. Synergy means that the whole is greater than the sum of the parts. The results together are greater than what each individual could achieve on their own. Now an important caveat to synergy is that it seems to me a lot of people these days are forgetting that, *You will only have a synergistic effect if everyone involved is giving their very best.*

Did you ever do any of those group projects in school? Of course, you did. I think we all have done them. I don't know about you, some of the people I know really loved them because they knew that other people on the team were going to pick up their slack. They thought *hey, I can take it easy.* And these people, because it affects their grade as well, will work extra hard and make sure that the work gets done.

I was the other kind of person. I was the one that wanted to be sure that my grades were good. So I would do the work that others wouldn't do. Here is the problem with this arrangement, the truth is the result was not as good as it would have been if every person had done their part and had committed to doing his or her best.

The same thing is true for you. So you first have to make a commitment that you're not going to slack off, that you are not going to take it easy - that you're not going to just get by - that you're not going to have that attitude that says well, it could be a lot better, it should be a lot better but this is good enough. You have to make the commitment that you will give your very best. Make a commitment that you will neither offer or accept any excuses. Let it start with yourself - that you will be a problem solver.

- Determine that you will figure it out and you will push through.
- Commit that you will be persistent so that you can give your very best and get the best results.
- Then be sure that you surround yourself with people who have that same kind of commitment.

It may be that you just start with one person. That is how it worked for me. I decided that if I could just find one more person with a common goal we could help each other.

Maybe they are further ahead of me or maybe they're just getting started. But they have a goal and they are willing. Be sure that the team you assemble has a strong work ethic. Surround yourself with people who have the commitment, the drive, the zeal, and the vision that will move you forward. What happens is as you do that? You level up. Your growth comes faster. Your capacity becomes greater. As you both excel more and more of the right people will be attracted to you. You will find your tribe of people and together you will go farther. You will do better. You will achieve more. It may be that you're the leader of that group. It is possible that someone else leads and you're a great supporter. If the leader is ready it is easy to be a great follower.

Find your role and then keep on keep on going. Keep on persevering. Keep on working together. You will achieve great things if you keep on doing it. There will be times when you will want to quit. There will be times where you feel like you can't go on. You may even say, "I can't do this anymore." Don't listen to yourself. Be sure that in those times, you talk to yourself. You don't focus on the pain. You don't focus on the challenge. You don't focus on the problems. You focus on your commitment. You focus on the big picture. Focus on what you want more than this temporary break. Focus on what you want more than this temporary pain. You keep on now. Focus on your WHY!

When you're looking for that tribe - I do think it's important to remind you of this - don't tell too many people. Especially early in the process. You may be saying, "How am I supposed to find other people to partner with, other people to be a part of my tribe? If I don't tell people?" There will be signs. Trust me. There will be signs. For me, I looked for other people that were running. I paid attention to the shoes they wore. If you're wearing a particular brand of shoes or a particular style of shoe, the chances were higher that you were a runner. I found people who were runners. Then I talked to them. I paid attention. I spent time with them and I developed that group. The same thing is true for you.

If you're committed to building your business, look for other people who are committed to building their business. If you're committed to hitting your goals, look for other people who are driven, who don't accept excuses, and pay attention to them. But if you tell too many people especially early, what you'll hear is all of the people who are negative. You will find all of the people who are saying you're crazy. You can't do that. They will say things like, *I tried it before. I couldn't. So you can't either.*

You will be discouraged. You don't need people to discourage you. Don't accept the discouragement. There is more than enough discouragement that will come naturally. Just like with running I learned to expect there to be a struggle. I've learned to expect there to be discouragement. I knew that there will be times where I hit the wall. There were times that I felt like I could not run any farther. I can't run any faster right now. Sometimes my endurance would go down, my speed would go down and I would want to just quit.

I expected that to be part of the training. I knew that when the alarm clock went off, there would be mornings - in fact, there were lots of the mornings - that I did not want to get up. I did not want to get ready and go out and run. Here's the secret – that is what it is most essential that you quit talking about it, you quit thinking about it and you just take action! Once you do. Once you break that gravitational pull of doing nothing, then everything changes. Once you start you will realize that this is better. I'm glad I did it. When you keep on you start getting the rewards!

As you select your tribe, be sure that you are looking for people who are ahead of you. You never want to be the smartest person in the room. You never want to be the best in the group. Honestly, that one is harder for me. I am naturally competitive. I loved to win. I'll make almost everything a competition. That is one of the reasons. GPS is dangerous when an expected travel and arrival time I take it as a personal challenge! That being said, it is still important to surround yourself with people that are ahead of you. They don't have to be way ahead of you. The truth is there are many reasons For you that it is better that they are not too far ahead.

I have run with people who are much faster than me. And those times there were several options that I had. I could run faster. That is a great strategy for a little while. When I did that, it did not take long for The to run far ahead of me. Even when I gave my very best effort, they were still faster than me. That was discouraging to me. It was discouraging, even though I remembered that I was really competing with myself. My goal was simply to be better today than I was yesterday. There were times that it was more than discouraging. There were times when running this way was damaging. Pushing myself harder than I had prepared for, and I had trained for resulted in setbacks and injuries. There are plenty of reasons people trained for long races.

There have been times when I was running with people who are much faster than me that I really struggled inside. There were all kinds of questions and accusations that ran through my mind. Why can't I? Will I ever? Why am I even doing this? My running became much harder because the people I was running with were so much better. Occasionally, I ran with people who were passionate about other kinds of running. Because of this I tried trail, running in the mountains and obstacle course races. Once again that did not work.

When I ran with people who were just a little bit better or faster than me I am constantly challenged in ways that are achievable. People who are a little head of me can remember what it was like people people who are far ahead of you have grown past it. People who are a little of are willing to invest in you and your growth because they have had someone do the same for them.

In your life and business, look for people who are only 10% ahead of you. Don't look for or ask for something for nothing. They may be willing, that's not the way a winner works. Since you see the value and learning from others who are ahead of you give it some value. They may not be money. be sure it is something. Find some way to give back. Maybe they will want you to pay it forward. Look for people that are better in specific ways. Maximize your strength, but don't forget your weaknesses.

Think about the way a head coach puts a coaching staff together. They surround themselves with people who have particular excellence. A football coach wants other coaches that are better at coaching specific positions than they are. On the team, not everyone has the same talent, skills, roles, or responsibilities. Build your team - your tribe - the same way! It is absolutely vital that you are intentional about the people you spend your time with. You will become like them!

If you hang around five smokers, you will be the sixth.

If you hang around five fit people, you will be the sixth.

If you hang around five confident people, you will be the sixth.

If you hang around five intelligent people, you will be the sixth.

If you hang around five goal oriented people, you will be the sixth. I

f you hang around five driven people, you will be the sixth.

If you hang around irresponsible people, you will be the sixth.

If you hang around, broke people, you will be the sixth.

Be sure to do this - *give yourself the win*. Give yourself the win that says I overcame myself. I broke through my own laziness. I overcame my own tiredness. You may struggle the whole time – we will talk about how you don't have to later - but at the end, you will be glad that you pushed through! You will be glad that you overcame. You will be glad that you took action. You will be glad that you did not accept your excuse.

One of the greatest things to do in this area is leverage yourself. Make it where you don't have a choice. "No matter what happens, I will do this!" The NO MATTER WHAT ATTITDUE is a necessity! It is one of my running lessons that had the greatest impact on all of my life. For a little over four years I ran every single day for at least a mile. I averaged three and a half miles a day. The thing I love the most about my run streak was the discipline that it brought not just in running but in everything. It didn't matter if I felt good. It did not matter if I wanted to. It didn't matter if it was convenient. It didn't matter what the weather was. It didn't matter if it was raining or snowing or there were sleet. It didn't matter if the wind was blowing. I knew this - no matter what - today, I'm going to run!

Once you have made this kind of commitment there is a key that makes it easier. If you're going to do something anyway, and it's something you don't want to do, just get up and get it done first.

Do the hard things first and Eat the Frog!

Do the hard thing first and then you've already got a win. When you start your day with a win you can keep on winning throughout the day. So leverage yourself. Reward yourself, tell yourself, I'm not lying to myself. I said I would do it. So no matter what I'm going to do it!" Please do not just say the words. If you say them without meaning them... if you say them without emotions – your brain knows it. Your brain will respond, *BULL! You are not going to do that.* So get up. Stand up. Speak up. Move your body. Put some intensity in your voice!

You may be saying, wait! What is this "Eat the Frog" business. Business guru Brian Tracy first introduced me to the concept. He says that if you know you have to eat a frog in the next 48 hours it is important to think about what you do. The common thing to do would be to put it off as long as possible. He suggested if you go this route you will spend the next two days dreading what you already know you have to do. Instead of running the next 48 hours, Brian Tracy suggest another route. Since you have already decided that you will eat the frog, do it first thing. Instead of running two days and then doing whatever it takes to get over it. When you do it first what you find out is that it probably was not as bad as you had imagined that it would be. And even if it was as bad or worse, now it is over!

More than talk

If you are serious about running your life you have to do more than talk. Write down what you are going to do. I write down the goal. I write down the discipline. Writing is better than thinking because you can think something and then not be serious. When you write it down it's like you made a contract with yourself. Then ask yourself, *Am I going to keep my word to myself?* This is where it gets even more serious. If you cannot trust yourself there are much bigger issues! If you have lied to yourself in the past think about this: If you will lie to yourself, why would you expect someone else to trust you? If you have a history of struggling to keep your word – this is a great time to start building your personal integrity. One day at a time, one action at a time, keep your word to yourself – NO MATTER WHAT! If it is late, keep your word. If you are tired, keep your word. If you forgot, keep your word. No lies. No excuses. No, putting it off – KEEP YOUR WORD!

Make it matter!

One of the greatest tools to help you keep your word is this. Write down what you are going to do. Make it specific. Then tape your promise and $100 bill to the mirror. If you do not do what you said you were going to do burn the money. Yes, you heard me right. Burn it. Don't give it away. Don't give it to some charity. Don't do something good with it. Burn the money. Now you may be saying that I am crazy. You may be right. Or maybe you have been crazy by saying that you are going to make a change and then just playing around with it. Here is what I know. Research has shown that people are motivated much more by a fear of loss than they are by the desire to win. You will do a lot more to keep yourself from burning $100 than you would to make $100. So when you've made the decision and you've thought it out you've written it down and you've made the commitment, sign the paper, then take one more step and tape $100 to the mirror. If losing $100 doesn't bother you, burn $200. If you fail again, add another one and burn $300. Figure out what it takes to keep your commitments. Leverage yourself to make the progress that you say you really want to make.

MAKE IT YOURS!
Chapter 2: Get a Partner

1 Who are the **five people** influencing me most right now—and what direction are they pulling my habits and mindset?

2 Where do I need **support and accountability** the most—and what kind of partner would actually help me win?

3 Am I being the kind of partner I want (work ethic, attitude, excuses)—or am I expecting others to carry me?

4 Who is **10% ahead of me** in the area I want to grow—and what is one way I can add value while learning from them?

5 What is one intentional step I will take this week to **build my tribe** (join, reach out, invite, schedule, commit)?

3

CELEBRATE EVERY WIN

Do you ever feel like it's not enough? No matter how hard you work, no matter how long you work, no matter how much progress you make, it's just really not enough. You are not alone. In fact, almost everyone feels this way at times. Social media makes it easy to play the comparison game. It really is not accurate to call it a game. Games are fun. That's why we choose to play them. This one is not fun. It leaves us feeling behind. It leaves us feeling inadequate. It leaves us feeling like we are not enough. What we do is not enough.

You wish you worked harder. You wish you had worked longer. You wish you would have made more progress. Sometimes it is obvious. Not only did you not make enough progress, you went backwards. One of the most important things I've learned is that it is vital to celebrate every win. It's hard to describe what a win is. When there is a constant struggle it is hard to feel like you are winning. Is the win only at the end of the journey? Does a goal have to be fully achieved before you can determine whether you won or lost?

I want to suggest to you a different mindset. Let me use my weight loss as the illustration. If you remember in chapter one I told you about the beginning of my running journey. At that time I had lost 20 pounds and weighed 255. I don't know about you, maybe you have dieted too. Maybe you struggled to diet. It seemed like for years, I started a new diet every Monday. I would start off well. Breakfast I was on point. Lunch I did well. When it was time for supper my commitment, desire, and willpower had worn thin. Supper time was always a challenge. My willpower had been used up from fighting myself all day. My desire to lose weight was diminished. The excuses and lying to myself about how it really was not THAT bad had grown during the afternoon. Sometimes I would give in. Sometimes I would stick to the plan. Even when I resisted there were so many days that I would step on the scales in the morning and there would be no progress. Some days there would be great progress. Then there were those days, you know the ones I'm talking about, the days where instead of losing weight, instead of maintaining, I gained weight. That's when it really got tough.

I was frustrated. I was disappointed. I would feel like giving up. You know the feeling. After struggling with that for years, I realized that I was doing it all wrong. Feeling bad about yourself and being disappointed all the time does not help you to overcome. Instead of making it better, it makes it harder to stay on track. What if instead of beating yourself up you celebrated your wins? Celebrate even if it did not show up on the scales.

When you make the hard choice - you really wanted to eat something off of the plan, you really wanted a Dr. Pepper, you really wanted a piece of cake or some ice cream that seemed to cry out unceasingly at night, when you said no to all of that – that is a serious win! I learned that if I overcame that urge, that one decision, This is worth celebrating! So I would celebrate! Celebration looked different. There were times I celebrated by physically patting myself on the back and telling myself, "You did well." In the mornings when I got on the scales and there was major progress, I would pump my arms in the air and celebrate I would say out loud, yes, enthusiastically. On the days when I just maintained I would celebrate that I didn't gain weight. Even on those days when I gained weight, I would celebrate that I wasn't where I used to be and that I'd made good decisions, and that something was going on but I was going to stay on course. Doing that made it possible for me to lose 100 pounds! It wasn't fast. It wasn't easy, but it happened.

It's important for you to focus on progress, not perfection. We are our own toughest critic. Even though we know better we expect absolute perfection. If we fall anywhere short of that, anything short of what we wanted, anything short of what we expected, we feel like it's an absolute failure. More than feeling like our effort was an absolute failure, we tell ourselves that we are failures.

There is a huge difference between failing and being a failure. The very fact that you are even reading this book, that you even care about improving your life, says that you are not a failure! You may have some failures, but you're not one. I want to encourage you today to make a decision that you're going to focus on progress, not perfection. If you made good decisions, if you took good actions, even when the progress is not as great as you want it to be, CELEBRATE that. CELEBRATE what you did.

In everything you do, there can be some win. One of the life-changing things I learned from running is that there is always a win! Even on the days that I had the worst run, I would remind myself, you got up, you ran, you did what no one else did. There are so many people who say I want to run or I want to get in shape. I want my life to change but they don't do anything about it. So even when it's hard, even when it's disappointing, even when you don't want to celebrate that you did something, even when the results are not as good as you expected them to be, celebrate that you got some kind of results.

You see, without victory, there is no survival. I want to say that again.

Without victory, there is no survival.

When you literally, not just in your mind but physically, celebrate the victory it gives you motivation! Celebrating gives you the fuel to make the next right choice. That is what you've got to do. Victory is not measured in miles but in inches. You went a little now and you hold your ground. The next time you went a little more. You do it decision by decision by decision, action by action by action, day after day after day, week after a week, month after month, year after year. It's a long journey in the same direction. If you're going to make the journey, if you're going to hit the goal, you've got to celebrate every win.

Right now, where are you beating yourself up? What are you frustrated about?

You are not alone. In fact, almost everyone feels this way at times. Social media makes it easy to play the comparison game. It really is not accurate to call it a game. Games are fun. That's why we choose to play them. This one is not fun. It leaves us feeling behind. It leaves us feeling inadequate. It leaves us feeling like we are not enough. What we do is not enough. Giving yourself the win is necessary for continued progress. That is why Dave Ramsey's debt snowball is so popular and effective. He frequently says some things that apply to so much more than finances.

Getting out of debt is not a mathematical problem, it's a behavior problem .

Personal finance is 80% behavior and only 20 .

There are a lot of strategies that make more sense , constantly.

Pay off your debt smallest to largest. Doing this causes you to get more traction. It brings wins faster. It builds momentum!

How will you apply these "Snow Ball" momentum truths to your life? Ramsey gives baby steps to winning financially. What are your baby steps.

What are the small actions you can begin and continue to practice that will make a difference in your:

Marriage
Parenting
Home Life
Work
Business
Faith

I want to encourage you to find something there to celebrate and give yourself every win. It really makes all the difference in the world.

MAKE IT YOURS!
Chapter 3: Celebrate Every Win

1 Where am I most likely to say, "It's not enough"—and how is that mindset affecting my motivation and consistency?

2 What counts as a "win" for me **before** the final result shows up—and what wins have I been ignoring?

3 Where am I confusing **failing** with **being a failure**—

and what would "progress, not perfection" look like this week?

4 What is one way I can build momentum using **small wins** (like a "snowball") in my health, finances, relationships, or work?

5 What is a win I can celebrate today—and how will I celebrate it in a way that fuels my next right choice?

4

BELIEVE YOU CAN

October 13, 2008 That date seems like a long time ago. It is a date that may have no meaning to you. If you are a Clemson Tiger football fan it is a very important date. On October 13th Terry Don Phillips, the athletics director of Clemson and Tommy Bowden, the head coach of the football team, sat next to each other in McFadden auditorium.

Bowden was a coach who had started the season with high hopes and big expectations. In his ten seasons at the helm of the Clemson football program Bowden had build what many considered a powerhouse. As the 2008 season began the goals were clear. Win the conference championship and contend for National Championship. Six games into the season those hopes, expectations and goals were a distant memory. On October 13th his team sat at 3-3 having suffered a humiliating defeat 4 days before.

The dismal start to the 2008 season left the team, coaching staff, fan base and university administration in disarray. It was clear that something had to change. Of course the coaching staff had been working on improving since spring practice began almost 8 months earlier. Finally a decision was made. Action was taken. That is why the A.D. and head coach were meeting in McFadden auditorium and the room was full of "interested parties."

It was time to make a change at the top of the football program. Yes, it was that bad. In the middle of the season Coach Bowden stepped down. This was the kind of thing that put the sports world on high alert. The questions started flying. Everyone had an opinion. What do you do? Who leads now?

There was a young assistant who had been on the staff for 5 years. Was he part of the problem? Was he part of the solution? Could he cover for the rest of the season? Was he ready? Ready or not, Dabo Swinney was named the interim head coach of the Clemson Tigers.

In his first meeting with the team Dabo Swinney had one sign made for the locker room. The sign was painted on the wall of the locker room. The sign was really just one word. BELIEVE. For Dabo it was the most important word. Everything depended on that word. What you believe. Why you believe it. What you do because of it.

Believe was more than some word for the remainder of a season. It is the word for the whole football program. It is a commitment. It is an approach. It is the value. It is the challenge. When Clemson lost the National Championship in 2017 the sign was there. When they started the nest season it was there. When they played Ohio State it was there. When Clemson prepared to play Alabama in 2017 the sign was still there. 'Bama came into that game having won 26 games in a row. They were the hands down favorite. Many said that this Alabama time was a NFL caliber team. It was argued that they could compete at the professional level. Yet that word, that one word, not a wish, not some dream or a mere hope was still the sign on the wall, the shirts, the hearts and minds of the Clemson Tigers football team. BELIEVE

At halftime of the 2017 National Championship game the Tigers found themselves trailing badly. The first half had not gone as anyone expected. The Crimson Tide was simply as good as everyone had been saying. As the Tigers assembled in the locker room Dabo's message to his team was simple. "I BELIEVE somehow we will win." Dabo was right! The Tigers did win! Why? They believed what their coach believed. "I BELIEVE somehow we will win."

One of the great lessons I learned from running applies to every part of your life. That lesson resulted in me dealing with my own limiting beliefs. Beliefs about whether I was able or not. If you remember the story of the beginning of my running, you remember that on the first day and on the second day that I followed my daughter, the thought occurred to me you should run with her. I remember laughing a little bit and looking down at my 255 pounds, period. I participated in athletics in high school, but I don't know that it would be accurate to say that I was an athlete.

There were times and there were sports that I was pretty good at. There were times and sports that you could even say that I was above average. But let's be clear - if you were listing great athletes, my name would not appear on the list. Now, 25 years later, my first thought was, "there is no way there's no way you can run." It was followed quickly by, "there is no way you can keep up. It's just impossible." That is why I want to remind you have how important having a compelling why is. The motivation was great enough for me to push back against those limiting beliefs. I was able to set aside for a moment the belief that I was not able to run that much or keep up. The next morning I had a plan. My plan was not to run for miles. The plan was simple. My plan was to run a little, then walk a little, then run away a little, then walk a little, then run a little, walk a lot, and then run some more.

I started going to the track in the afternoon and I would run the straights and walk the curves. I continued this until I became more comfortable. Here's an important point. I never waited until I was *completely* comfortable. To push myself further. There's something incredible about the way we are wired. If we ever get comfortable we begin to lose our intensity. We lose our drive. We lose our focus. We lose our desire. We kind of settle in. It's a comfort zone that can be so dangerous. So before I was comfortable running a full 100 meters, I started running 150 and then 200 and then 300, and then 400 or one lap. I ran two laps, then I ran three laps. I began to believe that I could run a mile and then two and then three. Whatever it is you're focusing on in your life, one of the most important things you can do is believe that you can.

Henry Ford is famous for a lot of things – the assembly line, the five day work week, doubling the pay of his factory workers and caring for the people who worked for him are just a few of his major initiatives. One of his most famous statements says this, "Whether you believe you can, or believe you cannot, you are right."

I wish I had said that long before Henry Ford because I believe it to the core of my being. Belief creates vision. Belief makes it possible for us to see into the future. Instead of waiting for life to happen to us, belief makes it possible for us to happen to life. Instead of just taking things as they come or seeing how it works out, make a decision and move in the direction of that decision. And the way we do that depends on our belief if we see that future we can get there. The beautiful thing about believing in vision is the closer you get to that vision, the clearer the vision becomes. The closer you get to your goal, the clearer it becomes and the more you're able to see what is ahead.

Back to my running analogy. When we ran on the streets there were times where I would look ahead and think I couldn't run anymore. I would tell myself just make it to the next street, or to the next stoplight or to the next stop sign. Just go a little further. When I got there, I would say, "do you really want to quit here? Or do you want to push further?" The same thing is true for you in business. The same thing is true for you in relationships. It is true in everything that matters.

I grew up going to motivational seminars for a business my father was involved in. I learned something in the early 1980's that has stuck with me ever since. "All you can do is all you can do and all you can do is enough!" I encourage you to memorize these words. Believe these words. Live these words! Realize this. All you can do matters. I hear people say "I have done EVERYTHING I can." I always think, and sometimes I ask, "have you really done EVERYTHING you can, or have you just given it some effort?" David Goggins says that when your mind tells that you are done – there is nothing more you can do you, you have only used 40% of your capacity!

Believe that you are capable.
Believe that you are strong enough.
Believe that you will figure it out.
Believe that you are worth it.
Believe that your dreams can be reality.
Believe.

In my coaching business I tell people frequently, "if you believed in you half as much as I believe in you, you would believe in you twice as much as you do!" It is interesting that it is easier for us to believe in others than it is to believe in ourselves. We can see other's capacity and doubt our own.

In business it is clear.

BIG GOALS require BIG ACTION.

You may be asking yourself, "is it possible?" The answer is YES! What does it require? Belief. Action. Attitude. Persistence. Adjustments. The same is true in your relationships.

Your belief creates vision. And as you move toward that vision, it becomes more clear and what is beyond it becomes clearer. You can get a glimpse of it and keep moving. Keep setting goals and going forward. Robert Dale has written a lot about what he calls the life cycle. He says that everything starts with a dream. As the dream grows you move to beliefs. From your beliefs you set goals. Your goals require structure in order to be realized. The structures make it possible for the dream to become a reality. Dale goes on to teach that if you do not dream a new dream you will start to decline. This starts with nostalgia where you reminisce about how things used to be. Nostalgia digresses into a period of questioning where you become suspicious about others and what is going on in the world, your family or business. Questioning slides down into polarization. Finally polarization leads people to drop out or just quit.

I hope from this it is clear how important it is to believe. Belief creates strength of will. Belief is very different from just hoping or dreaming. That is not what we're talking about. What I'm talking about is believing. Being certain to the core of your being that you can. This kind of knowing gives you a strength of will. It helps you not to listen to yourself but to talk to yourself. You resist that 40% rule and strongly encourage yourself - *I can! I will! I will accomplish it!*

It creates a strength of will that keeps you going when you don't want to go on.

When you don't feel like you can go on your belief, your commitment and your desire will keep you going. Why is it important to believe that you can? Because belief creates resilience. It's not a perfect journey. Running is not perfect. Businesses not perfect. Relationships are not perfect. Nothing is perfect. I hear people say very often if everything works out, I'm going to do this or do that. I chuckle to myself and sometimes even say it out loud, "*Nothing ever goes right all of the time.*" The question is not will it be perfect? The question is what are you going to do about it? The answer depends on your belief!

There will be challenges, but your belief creates resilience. You will get knocked down. There will be set backs. There will always be things that are outside of your control. You should fully expect there to be pressure. Your belief in the 'future you', your belief in your capacity, and your belief in achieving the goal in front of you, will get you back up. It will move you forward.

Why is it important to believe you can? Because belief ignites and activates. Your belief will get you out of bed in the morning. Your belief would get you started when you don't want to start. Your belief is a fire inside of you. This is why I believe I can and I will.

MAKE IT YOURS!
Chapter 4: Believe You Can

1 What is the "there's no way I can" thought I keep hearing—and where did that belief come from?

2 What would change if I acted like Henry Ford's quote is true: **my belief is shaping my outcome**?

3 What is a goal that requires me to **expand my identity**—who do I need to become to achieve it?

4 What is the smallest "run a little / walk a little" step I can take to prove to myself that growth is possible?

5 When my mind says "I'm done," what is one phrase I will use to **talk to myself** instead of listening to myself?

5

TRAINING PLAN

I love sports. I love to participate and spectate. I want to take you on an imaginary journey. Just imagine you go to a basketball game. The whole arena is completely full. The teams have warmed up. The National Anthem has been played. The starting five for each team has been announced. The players get set. the official throws the ball into the air for the tip-off. The team with the ball dribbles to their end of the court and gets ready to run a play when all of a sudden they notice that the goals have been removed. The point guard stops dribbling. He looked at the other players and the coach. Confusion fills everyone's face and mind. No one knew what to do because there are no goals.

How often have you lived your life that way? You plan. You prepare. You get ready. You start. But you have no goals. Goals are absolutely important. There is a great illustration from the old story of Alice in Wonderland. Alice is wandering aimlessly. She is lost. Finally she encounters a cheshire cat at a fork in the road. She asks the cat which path to choose. The cat responds, "where do you want to go?" "I don't know," Alice answered. Then the cat says, "if you don't know where you're going, any road will take you there."

It is not uncommon for people to just wander aimlessly through life to fall into the monotony of getting up and going to work. Taking care of a few things after work, going to bed falling asleep. waking up the next morning to the alarm clock and doing it all over again. No progress is made.

It's one step forward, two steps back, go to the right go to the left turn around. One of the things I learned from running that changed my business and my life is it's important to have a training plan when you're preparing to do something big and when you're preparing to do something that you've never done before. You don't just all of a sudden start. No one goes to Mount Everest on their first day and climbs to the top. In fact, if you've researched that at all, most people spend years training before they actually start climbing. It looks like they have not started when they're at the foot of the mountain. The truth is, if you have not done the work beforehand, you have just started and you are destined to fail. If you have put in the work before, then you have got a shot. The thing that makes the difference between having a shot and actually doing it is having a training plan.

So whatever you're working on, whatever the plan or the goal, it is it's important to have multiple steps along the way. They must be strategic. They must build on one another. When I first decided to run a 5k I did not simply start off running 3.1 miles. I started off wanting to run one-quarter mile without stopping. The next step was a half mile. Then the goal was one mile, then two, then three. My strategic plan did not just include running. There was also cross-training. I planned to do things that did not appear to directly affect running. These activities were vitally important. My plan extended beyond exercise. The plan included what I ate. My plan determined how much sleep I got. My plan determined how I took care of my body. This is a point that many people miss. You are a whole person. We act like we can focus on one aspect of our lives and it will not affect the rest either positively or negatively. It is not true. You have one life. What you do in one area will affect all the rest. You can live with an over-emphasis for a while. It will not take long for the neglect in the other parts of your life to show up. How many people do you know who have been so focused on their career that they let important relationships suffer? Have you ever sacrificed your health in pursuit of something?

I want to be clear. I am not suggesting that you can or even should live a balanced life. I know a lot of people work hard to keep life in balance. They talk about being out of balance. I do not believe that your life will ever be balanced. Of course I have had people resist this premise. I usually ask them to define what balance means. Does it mean that you give equal amounts of time, energy, attention, effort and focus to each area. Does it mean that you work 40 hours a week and spend 40 hours a week with your family? Does that carry on to say that you give 40 hours a week to your faith? Be sure to sleep 40 hours a week as well. Then do you give 40 hours a week to your physical fitness? Of course not. There are only 168 hours in a week.

Balance is not the goal. For me the goal is living according to my values, goals and priorities. Practically that means there are times when I give more time, energy, attention, effort and focus to one area without letting the others suffer. There are weeks when I spend a lot more time working. There are weeks when I invest a lot more time with my family. It is not balance, it is living according to my priorities.

A complete strategic plan is a necessity. A goal without a plan is just a wish. Too many of us wish we were this or wish we were that. We wish we could accomplish this or wish we accomplished that. The problem is that we don't have a plan. The result is that we make no progress. One of the beautiful things about the world we live in now is there are all kinds of training plans. And there are all kinds of apps. Some of them actually tell you exactly what to do. That is not always helpful because life and business don't necessarily fit a one-size-fits-all approach. You can use those resources and tools to write it down. They can serve to give yourself reminders and to keep you moving in the right direction. When you have got the plan and you know step by step, then it is time to make a commitment.

Unless you make a strong commitment your plan ends up being only empty promises and hopes. Plans and commitment must be something like this - I will do this no matter what. No matter what is the difference maker! I promise there will be days you wake up and you will not feel like it. There will be days when you have no motivation. If you depend on motivation alone, then you cannot make it. You need motivation. You need a plan. You need a commitment to go along with it that says I will do this. Even when I don't feel like it, I will do this even when I don't think it's making any difference. I will do this when I don't feel like I'm making any progress. I am committed to working on the plan and taking the steps that will get me to the place I want to go.

When you're working on your plan, remember this, No Man, and No Woman is an island. You don't have to do it alone. You live in a time where it is so easy to access others who've already accomplished what you want to do. And if you're not surrounding yourself with people of like minds who have similar goals, you're cheating yourself out of an incredible advantage. Be a person who is selective about who you spend your time with and how you spend that time. Ask questions. Be inquisitive. Pay attention to what others do. Then imitate them.

Tom Landry, the famous Dallas Cowboys football coach said, "Setting a goal is not the main thing. It's deciding how you will go about achieving it and staying with that plan. That's the main thing."

> "Setting a goal is not the main thing. It's deciding how you will go about achieving it and staying with that plan. That's the main thing."

SETTING a goal is not the main thing. It is deciding how you will go about achieving it and staying with that plan that makes a difference. It's important to remember when you are following your plan, that progress and growth are not linear. It's not consistent upward.

There will be days when you feel like you're further behind. There'll be days when you feel like you're not making progress. And then there will be times when you will have huge jumps in my running. I watched my pace and my distance every single day. And I always wanted to run further and to run faster. The problem with that is pushing yourself to maximum capacity every single day ends up limiting your capacity. You have to be strategic in your plan. In running that meant that there were days when I pushed harder in running. There are days where I ran a lot faster than I did on other days. It meant that there are days that I run a lot further than I did on other days. Realizing that the progress is not linear, helped me keep on.

So what's your plan? What is your goal? Do you know where you want to go? Do you know who you want to be? Are you clean on what you want to achieve? What do you want to have? Do you know the steps that will move you in that direction? Are you willing and committed to taking those steps consistently? What is your pace?

You have to have a training plan!

MAKE IT YOURS!
Chapter 5: Training Plan

1 What am I trying to do that's big—and where am I attempting it without a real plan?

2 If my goal is the destination, what are the **milestones** I need between here and there (quarter mile → half mile → one mile)?

3 What "cross-training" areas (sleep, food, mindset, relationships, structure) will directly affect my success even if they seem indirect?

4 Where do I confuse "balance" with "priorities"—and what would it look like to align my week with my true priorities?

5 What is my plan for the days when progress isn't linear—when I feel slow, stuck, or behind?

6

MAKE TIME

How many times have you said, *"I would love to do that?"* *"Whenever I find time I would love to help you but I just don't have the time."* *"I would love to start this but I don't have the time."*

One of the life-transforming lessons I learned from running is that time will never accidentally appear. You have to make time. If you've never thought about it, let's start with this... have no doubt about it, time is the most precious resource you have. It is easy for us to live like money is the most valuable resource we have. The truth is you can make more money. Of course, no one ever feels like they have enough money. We can always use more. We can always spend more.

There are always things to do. It is easy to spend money. So you don't have enough money. The same thing is true about time. You never have enough time and money. How many times have you said, *"I wish I had just another hour or two in the day?"* If you did get an extra hour or two each day, what would you do with it? When we say this or something like it we have BIG plans, dreams and goals. If I had an extra hour I would be so much more productive. I would get so much more accomplished. I would have time to do this. I would have time to spend with them. The reality is that you would use the extra time the same way you are presently using the time you have. Be honest. What percent of your 24 hours in a day are you actually focused and devoted? How well are you using and utilizing the 168 hours a week that you have presently?

The difference between time and money is when you spend money you can make more when your time is gone, it is gone. Forever. You cannot make more time. You only have what you have.

One of the most important things I learned was that there are opportunities that only come one time or for a limited time and when they are gone, they are gone. So much has been written about time management. And I think a completely different approach. I don't think the challenge is time management. It's really self management. Let me reemphasize a point I made earlier. Time management is a misnomer. We cannot manage time. The key is to manage ourselves. The hardest person to lead is yourself. If you really want to make progress in the area of time you need to be intentional. You need to manage yourself and your time based on your values, goals and priorities.

The first challenge in self management is being clear about what our values are. In my coaching practice I lead many of my clients through a values discussion that leads to values discovery. Frequently they say, "of course I know my values." When I ask them to write them down they are stuck. Test it yourself. In the space below write your 5-7 core values.

1.
2.

3.
4.
5.
6.
7.

The second step is to be clear on your goals. Jim Collins has made BHAG goals popular. A BHAG (Big Hairy Audacious Goal) is your 25 year goal. It is the vision for where you see your life going. 25 years may be challenging for you to envision. Start with at least 10 years. Then break that down to 3-5 years. What are your goals for this year? Use the space below to write out your goals for the year.

BASED on your values and goals, what are your priorities. It is helpful for me to think about my priorities in regards to the major components of my life. I focus on seven aspects. Faith. Family. Finances. Fitness and Health. Career. Intellect. Friends. It may be helpful to use the chart at the end of this chapter.

TAKE some time to be clear about the quality of life you want in each area and what it will be like when you are living life at that level. Describe that life in as much detail as possible. What are the things you will do to make the dream become the reality?

This approach is what makes it possible for you to "make time."

We can't make time speed up, and we cannot make time go slower. W hat we must do is literally determine what we are going to do with our time. Stephen Covey uses an illustration in his book, The Seven Habits of Highly Effective

People. He starts with a glass jar that is almost completely full of rocks. In the illustration, he arranges the rocks and gets a few more and then he asks the audience that he is presenting to if the jar is full. Most of them say yes. Then he will take a jar of gravel and begin to pour it into the larger jar. As he pours in the gravel he shakes things around and shifts the jar so that the gravel gets down between the crevices of the rocks. Then he asks the next question *"Does anyone want to change your answer?"* Of course people say, *"okay, I thought it was full but now I know it wasn't full." "So what about now?"* he asks. *"Is the jar full now?"* Some will say yes and some will say no. Then Covey pulls out sand and pours it in. The sand goes in, and it fills in more and more of those spaces. Finally he takes water and pours it in. After he's made this visual illustration he asks another question. *"What's the lesson that you learn from this?"* Inevitably, someone will say, *"no matter how full your life is, there's always room for more. "*

Have you ever fought that? Have you ever said it? Have you ever felt it?

Of course! I think we all do. Covey says it is the wrong point. The real point is what would happen if you fill the jar up with water and then added sand. The sand being more dense would displace the water. You'd still have water in the jar but the rest of the jar will be full of sand. The problem? When you attempt to put gravel or rocks in you would not be able to get them in because the jar would be completely full of water and sand. Covey says the real point is if you don't get the rocks in first, you never get them in.

If you don't get the rocks in first, you never get them in!

The rocks represent the big things. The rocks are the important things in our lives. The rocks are your priorities.

Covey also illustrates this approach with four quadrants. At the top are things that are important, and below the line are things that are unimportant. To the left are things that are urgent, and to the right are things that are not urgent. This quadrant helps us to see when we have all kinds of pressure. How often is your life too busy? Yes, it's true. We all have too many things to do. Realize that not every opportunity is your opportunity. Not every request or demand on my time or your time is really valid. We have to decide what's above the line and really important and what's not important. Then there's a pressure to always do the things that are urgent. The urgent leaves us always running from one crisis to the next and it controls our life.

Have you ever had one of those days where you feel like all you've done is gone from one problem to the next to the next to the next? At the end of the day, you are exhausted. As you evaluate the day you felt like you never really made any progress. That's because we've let the urgent push out the truly important.

In addition to Covey's four quadrants, I would add the third dimension. What is the third dimension? I am glad you asked! What is significant? Is it important or not? Is it urgent or non-urgent? Then is it significant? Will this action, this use of time, energy, resources and effort make a difference now and in the days to come? That gives it significance.

Have you ever thought about how life really works? Your life today is the result of the things you did or did not do 90-120 days ago. That is the significance factor. Think about weight loss as an illustration. In my "Get Fit and Never Quit" program the participants are often frustrated. They want to see IMMEDIATE results from the changes in their eating and exercising program. I remind them that their present state was not an immediate change. For many it took years to get into the condition that drove them to say I MUST CHANGE THIS. One day will not produce dramatic results. One week will not produce dramatic results. It took time to get into this condition and it will take time to change it. Giving up will not make it happen any faster.

Running taught me this time lesson. If it's important to me, and I made that decision that it would be, then it's something I'm going to do. If I control my time, then I will always be able to get it in. Missing one run may or may not make a difference today. Beyond a doubt it does make a difference in the long term. Here's the truth, whether it's running, exercise, whether it's your diet, whatever it is, your relationships, your business- If it is important, you will make the time and if it is not, you will make an excuse.

> **If it is important, you will make the time and if it is not, you will make an excuse.**

You see the truth about every one of us is that we make time for the things that are really important to us. If it is important, you just do whatever it takes. You work harder, you work longer, you work more efficiently. You ask for help when you need to. You do whatever it takes to get it done.

If it's not important to you...

If it's not a priority to you...

It's so easy to just make an excuse.

Excuses come in lots of forms. Excuses seem to all have similar formats. I ran out of time I didn't get to it. Something else came up. On and on the list goes. Maybe you find yourself looking for the perfect time. I'd like to start this business. I'd like to grow in this way. I'd like to do this thing. But this is not the perfect time. The truth is there's never a perfect time. There is only time. Since this is true, you, yes you, decide how to use the time you have. This running lesson has transitioned over into everything. I'm not suggesting that you have to do it this way. For me what it meant was I started getting up earlier. My wife actually started it. Before she started getting up at five o'clock in the morning. I thought there is no way in the world I will ever do that. As I developed the habit, and as the importance became more and more clear, I started getting up earlier and earlier and earlier, day after day after day. That changed a lot of things in my life.

Now our alarm clock usually goes off around 4:00 in the morning. I get up and get it done. That way, whatever comes up during the day does not have the ability to keep me from doing one of the things that I have decided is most important for the day. There have been times when I didn't get it done early. The temptation was so strong to just skip it. As strong as the temptation was, the commitment was even stronger. So start early or stay late. Do whatever it takes to get it done. That's the fundamental at the bottom of all of this. I'm asking you to adopt a **no matter what mentality**! No matter what happens, I will do the things that are most important.

No matter what happens. I will take care of the things that I've said are a priority in my life. No matter what happens. No excuses. No letting myself off the hook. No, saying I'll get back to it later. No. Adopt a no matter what mentality. what that requires is for you to slow down long enough to figure out what really is important in your life. Too many people have come to some important point in their life, only to realize that they did not focus on the things that are most important.

In my 34 years of coaching people, here are some of the things that I've never heard anyone say: *I wish I would not have done this.* I have never heard anyone say: *I wish I would not have made faith such a priority.* I've never heard anyone say: *I wish I never would have made my family such a priority.* I have never heard anyone say: *I wish I would not have made my fitness such a priority.* Are those on your list? What else is on your list? What is it really important for you to focus on and to make a commitment that you will get done?

No matter what.

MAKE IT YOURS
Chapter 6: Make Time

1 What do I keep saying I "don't have time for"—and what does that reveal about my real priorities?

2 What are the "rocks" in my jar right now—and what keeps displacing them (sand, gravel, urgent stuff, distractions)?

3 Where am I letting the **urgent** push out the **important**—and what boundary do I need to set?

4 What is one significant action (90–120 day payoff) I can schedule this week that my future self will thank me for?

5 What does "no matter what" need to look like in my calendar—what exact time and plan will make follow-through inevitable?

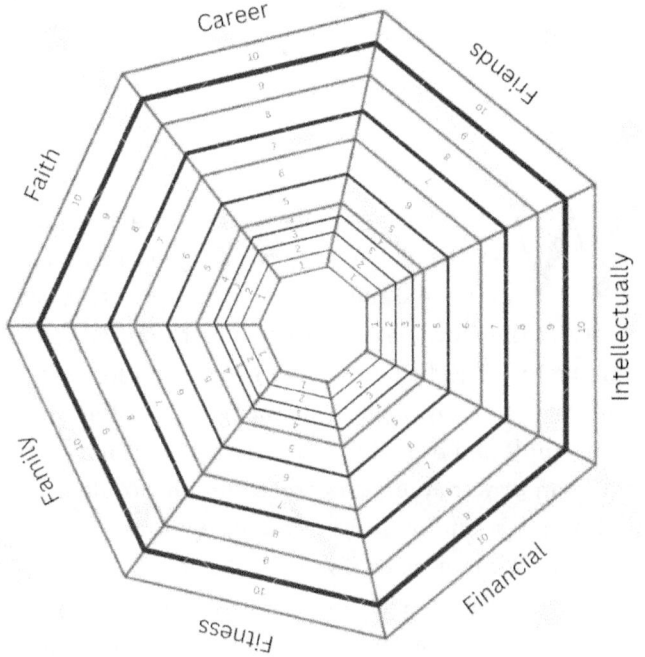

7

GOALS

When I first started running, my goal was simply to be able to keep my daughter in view while she did her cross-country practices at six o'clock in the morning. If you remember the story, she was running for miles by herself, and I started off following her in my suburban my progression was to drive to the corner of the first mile and run till I could see her then run back to my suburban drive to the next corner, run till I could sear run back to my suburban drive to the next corner repeat until we'd done the four miles. As soon as I started, I had a goal in mind and it was to be able to run the whole time and keep her in view. That was my big goal. Inside of it. I had a lot of little goals. The first one was to be able to run the straight and walk the curves on the track and continue to build up until I was able to run one mile without stopping. And then it was two miles. And then the goal was three miles and four and five and six, and then 13 and then 26.

Running taught me that I did better when I knew what I was running for, and I had a goal to work towards. I constantly signed up for races, I was challenging myself to run longer to run further. To run faster. And they weren't always the same. Sometimes it was just about the amount of time I ran. Sometimes it was about the distance sometimes it was about how fast I ran. And I found I did the best when I was in training for a specific race.

You see goals are vital and yet so many of us live our lives with no goals. If you went to any kind of sporting event and there was not a goal. It would not take very long for people to stop playing the game because without a goal you are simply just playing a game so how about you? Are you playing a game with your life? Are you actually living your life on purpose?

Earl Nightingale says, "Success is the progressive realization of a worthy goal or ideal."

I encounter so many people who are struggling in their lives. As I talk to them, one of the things I discover is that without a worthy goal, our lives fall into a monotonous rut where we get up and do the same thing. Day after day after day, week after week after week, month after month after month, year after year after year. And although we try not to ask why am I doing this? Why am I giving this effort? The monotony gets to us and we ask What is all of this for why am I doing it? And the real heart of the problem is we don't have a goal. We're not working towards something we don't have. something that excites us. something that keeps us going when it's hard. something that says you know it's worth it.

Norman Vincent Peale said, "All successful people have a goal."

No one can get anywhere unless he knows where he wants to go. And what he wants to be or do.

Many years ago, right after we were first married, my wife and I moved to the Metroplex of Texas. The Dallas Fort Worth area was new and exciting. We both grew up in relatively small places. And it was so exciting to have so many things to do and so many places to go and so very often on the weekend, we would literally just drive around to become familiar with the area and see what all was there.

That's fine for a day or two. But it's no way to live a life and if you're taking a trip if you're trying to go somewhere, instead of wandering around and hoping that you finally get there. It's much better to have a plan. This was back in the days of a map and so we would get out the map when we planned a trip and we'd find the best routes and we would see what was there, and what we wanted to see experience and do along the way. And in our day, it's easy to pull up your GPS on your phone and plot a destination and have multiple routes that guide us. Well, that's a great illustration of our lives because when we have the goal, when we have the destination in mind, even if we get off track, even if there's something happens and the car breaks down or you get a flat tire you need to do something different.

It is easy to recalculate get back on track and make progress toward the goal. Goals are vitally important, and if you don't have a goal stop reading right now. As much as I want you to read this book. More than that, I want you to stop and ask yourself, Where is my life going? What am I doing? What am I wanting to do? There is something that's better than goals. And that's habits. James is clear in his book Atomic Habits, and he talks about how habits are better than goals. Those goals require this motivation, but habits are about discipline and discipline is better than motivation. Motivation comes and goes and sometimes you're excited and sometimes you're tired, but when you discipline yourself and you form a habit of doing the things consistently, they get you to the place you want to be they cause you to be the person that does those things. Then you've really got the trump card you got the secret to becoming that person and achieving the things you want. I heard clear speaking on this point, and what he said is goals are great for people who want to win once.

Habits are great for people who want to win consistently. What did you think about that statement? Do you really want to win consistently then yes, set a goal. But then stop and say what are the steps that will get me to the goal? What kind of person do I need to be? What are the things that need to be in my life consistently for me to be that person and to achieve those goals and make those your habits? This is the time where you get down to very small things. For me, when I was running, I had to make the decision every night. I had to decide what time I would get up, and the process of how I would get up. I would get dressed. I would do a little bit of reading, and then I would go run. I made the decision the night before how far I would run, and how long I would run, and every day that I did that changed who I was.

Clear says it this way,

Every action you take is a vote for the person you wish to become.

If you've never read his book, I encourage you to put it on your reading list. One of the things he says is that it is about being and not doing. If you were changing your eating habits and someone offered you let's say a piece of cake, you could say, *Oh no, I thank you but I'm not going to eat that I'm on a diet.* But that's the doing if you focused on being what you would say is, *I appreciate you offering this but I don't eat desserts.* Or the illustration he uses is of a person who stopped smoking. And if someone offered that person a cigarette. You could say, *No thanks. I'm quitting smoking.* But the habit that forms the being would say this, *I'm not a smoker.* It's about your personal identity.

Habits are vitally important, and they get us further, faster, and more consistently to the destination than just having goals. It is so important to remember that you get what you repeat. After I'd been running for about a year, I was in a group setting and there was a discussion. I said I was a runner, and my next-door neighbor was in the group. And strangely, she said, *you're not a runner, right? You don't look like a runner.* Then about six weeks later, she came and apologized and she said, *you know it really struck me as strange when you said that. But as I've watched you over the last six weeks running away from your house and then after 30-45 minutes or an hour seeing you run back. As I've seen you running all over town. You've arrived. I didn't recognize it, but you are a runner, because that's what you do consistently.*

So let me ask you a question. What do you do consistently? Because what you do consistently, the habits that you place in your life, are either building you up, making you better, stronger, more resourceful changing your identity, or your habits that are tearing you down, are either moving you closer to the person you want to be or they're taking you further away from the person you want to be in your personal life. What are the habits that you've made? And what are the habits that you need to make in your business? What habits do you have? What steps do you take consistently to cause you to grow, to build your business stronger? And what are the habits that you've got that slow you down? Goals are important. The habits are even more important.

. . .

MAKE IT YOURS!

Chapter 7: Goals

1 If someone asked, "Where are you headed?" what is my honest answer—and is that destination acceptable to me?

2 What is one **worthy goal** that excites me enough to stay with it when it's hard?

3 What habit would make this goal almost unavoidable—what can I repeat daily/weekly that becomes a "vote" for the future me?

4 What identity statement do I need to adopt (example: "I'm not a smoker" / "I don't eat desserts")—and what identity have I been reinforcing instead?

5 What is one "race" I should sign up for (a deadline, commitment, public target) that forces action and consistency?

8

FIGHT

The name Jim Whittaker may not mean anything to you yet. Jim Whittaker was the first American to climb Mount Everest. If you're not familiar with climbing Mount Everest, it is a task that cannot be taken lightly. As of the writing of this book, 322 People have died as they attempted to climb Mount Everest. Mount Everest stands 29,032 feet at its peak. It is something that takes years of preparation to achieve. After conquering Mount Everest Jim Whittaker decided he would help other people train and experience what comes from accomplishing such an incredible task.

When you're as he's preparing his team to begin the ascent to the peak, a newspaper reporter was there interviewing those who are going and finally takes a chance to interview Whitaker. And he asked him, w*hy would people go through so much time and effort to spend so much money and go through such physical exertion just to climb this mountain?* With her paused and looked at him with a strange look on his face, and then he responded this way, *It is clear, sir, that you* *have never seen the view from the top of the mountain.* The interviewer waited and waited and waited.

He thought surely Whitaker would say something else. But as far as Whittaker was concerned, that was the end of the interview, the view from the top of the mountain. I don't know if you've ever thought about it, but the saying is true. No one at the top of the mountain got there accidentally. One of the things that running taught me was that I was too casual in my approach to life. I had some things I dreamed of achieving and dreamed of having and doing and even being and I thought I would get there someday. It would just happen. But what I found myself doing was just kind of floating through life dealing with this problem and that problem. Occasionally opportunities would come, and some of them I could take and some of them I was not ready for. As I started running, I discovered that being intentional and fighting through my own weakness, my own excuses, my own challenges, were key to a quality of life that I'd never experienced before.

The truth is that most of us are too soft. So many of the things that we call blessings, although they are great to enjoy, really serve to make us softer. We're not willing to work hard, we're not willing to think, we're not willing to sweat. I can remember even saying I've done all the sweating I want to do in my life. So if something was difficult, I just stopped. If it was hard and I wasn't sure it was worth it. Why give the effort? I mean what difference is it going to make my life's not great, but it's not too bad. And so in business, I look back now and wonder *what could have been if I had been more intentional, if I had been stronger, if I had fought through the difficult times, and the difficult problems in relationships. I wonder how would my relationships be different. If I would have been more willing to do the difficult things in my physical health?*

I have no doubt when I was 42 years old, I suffered an injury to my back, that was so severe I ended up in a wheelchair. I did all of the treatments to avoid surgery and finally had surgery. And I was told, *you will never run again. You will never ride a motorcycle again.* Even after the surgery I had excruciating pain and was not capable of doing what I'd done before. If you asked me what happened? I could have given you the short answer of the very moment but it literally was the straw that broke the camel's back.

The truth is that I had been soft and I'd been patient and not fought through my urges to eat whatever I wanted to eat. I was unwilling to exercise and take care of my body. Keep my muscles strong. And that is why I suffered the injury. The event was just the last straw. How about you? Are you soft? What are you willing to fight for and what are you willing to give up? One of the other things that running taught me in regards to finding, is I have been too patient. I may need to pause for a moment and tell you that everyone who knows me well would challenge that statement. In fact, some people have told me that I'm the most impatient person they have ever met. I understand what they mean. When I made the decision. I want it to happen right now. But there was the key. I had not made a decision. And so I thought, *Someday I will do this someday. I will become that someday. I will deal with this someday. I will make this effort someday it will be better.* But I was not willing to do what it took today.

There is a huge difference between Sunday and today. So here's what I want to encourage you to do. Work hard for what you want, because it won't come to you without a fight. One of my mentors John Maxwell says, *Everything worth-*

while is uphill. He's right. There is a fight and it's uphill. If it really matters to you, you will prepare and you will make an effort and you will keep on day after day after day. Making progress and climbing the hill. Getting better, getting stronger, becoming more resilient. In this fight for your health, for your business, for your relationship, for whatever it is, you want to have whatever it is, you want to do whatever it is you want to become.

You have to be strong and courageous and know that you can do anything you put your mind to. Now that may sound like some psycho-psychological mumbo jumbo, but it is true. You can have anything in life, but you can't have everything in life. Most of what you really want and yes, you have to purify that and make a decision. But most of what you really want is attainable. It just requires extreme amounts of effort. Grant Cardone has become famous for talking about ten times. That you should make your goals ten times larger than they are, that you should expect them to require ten times more than what you expect, that you should work ten times harder, and it will take ten times longer, and it will cost you ten times more.

He's not wrong. It really matters to you. You do what it takes you fight through first yourself and then it's easier once you've won the victory with yourself to win victories. With everyone and everything else. When you're doing this, understand that if someone puts you down or criticizes you, you just keep on believing in yourself and turn that into something positive. Use it as fuel for the fire that says you may have been right about my past, but you are not right about my present and you are not right about my future. And people around who discourage you. Yes, they're a big challenge. But the biggest war you ever go through is right between your own ears. It's in your mind. John Gordon says that we have to learn to talk to ourselves, not listen to ourselves. And you have to train your mind you have to take every thought captive and literally push it out the negative the questions that doubt. Push those aside.

Don't even give them room to echo in your heart and mind. Get rid of them. David Goggins, who is famous for extreme athletics doing extreme sports, running ultra marathons, and unbelievable feats, says *we are all going through a war in our mind, and we have to callus our mind to fight that war, and to win that war.*

We have to take those voices and quiet them. And my lead talks about the days of a CD and you get to have a CD and it would be playing. and sometimes when we get in that zone, it's like we've put a CD and we know we know the voice. We know what it says, we know the questions and the fear and the doubts that it creates. And the way to change the CD is you take it in and you take a pen, something sharp, a knife or something and you just scratch across the CD. and as you scratch back and forth, what happens is when you get to that when you get to that script that runs in your heart and mind that brings all those negative emotions. When you scratch through it, it just skips, and it jumps that part because it can't read the laser disc anymore.

What are the messages you've got? To quiet? You've got to stop listening to they are worth the fight. The physical limitations are worth the fighting the doubt from yourself and others. It's worth the fight to overcome it. How do you do it? You focus on the go. You create the habits. You make time you develop a plan. You believe that you can you celebrate every win along the way. You find a group of people who will support and encourage you and you don't stop no matter what happens.

. . .

MAKE IT YOURS!

Chapter 8: Fight

1 Where have I been "too soft"—choosing comfort over growth—and what has that softness cost me?

2 What is worth fighting for right now (health, marriage, business, calling)—and what would giving up lead to?

3 What is the mental battle I keep losing (doubt, excuses, comparison, quitting early)—and what is my strategy to win it?

4 When I hit the wall, what will I do instead of quitting—what is my pre-decided response?

5 What will I use as fuel (criticism, setbacks, pain, fear) to keep moving—and what does "everything worthwhile is uphill" mean for me personally?

ABOUT THE AUTHOR

Ray Young is husband, father and grandfather. He is a speaker, leadership coach and trainer. Ray is a real estate investor and operates several successful businesses.

Ray's life changed when he started running. The lessons he learned from running changed his life and the way he conducts business. You do not have to be a runner for this book to impact your life. You do have to apply these lessons. This short book will impact your life in profound ways the second you put the principles to work!

rayyoungspeaker.com

facebook.com/ray.young2
instagram.com/4ray2

www.ingramcontent.com/pod-product-compliance
Lightning Source LLC
Chambersburg PA
CBHW070408230526
45471CB00006B/2699